THE ST. LEONARD CHRONICLES

Other Plays by Steve Galluccio

In Piazza San Domenico

Mambo Italiano

Published by Talonbooks

THE ST. LEONARD CHRONICLES

A PLAY BY

STEVE GALLUCCIO

TALONBOOKS

Talonbooks
278 East First Avenue, Vancouver, British Columbia, Canada V5T 1A6
www.talonbooks.com

First printing: 2015
Typeset in Arno

Printed and bound in Canada on 100% post-consumer recycled paper
Interior and cover design by Typesmith
Cover illustration by Lester Smolenski

Talonbooks gratefully acknowledges the financial support of the Canada Council for the Arts, the Government of Canada through the Canada Book Fund, and the Province of British Columbia through the British Columbia Arts Council and the Book Publishing Tax Credit.

LIBRARY AND ARCHIVES CANADA CATALOGUING IN PUBLICATION

Galluccio, Steve, 1960–, author
The St. Leonard chronicles / Steve Galluccio.

A play.
Issued in print and electronic formats.
ISBN 978-0-88922-930-3 (PBK.).—ISBN 978-0-88922-931-0 (EPUB)

I. Title.

PS8563.A456S35 2015 C812'.6 C2014-907425-5
C2014-907426-3

The St. Leonard Chronicles premiered at the Centaur Theatre in Montreal, October 1 to November 3, 2013, then was remounted November 19 and extended to December 8, 2013, with the following cast and crew:

TERRY	Christina Broccolini
ROBERT	Guido Cocomello
CARMINE	Michel Perron
GINA	Dorothée Berryman
ELISA	Ellen David
DANTE	Vittorio Rossi
DORA	Jocelyne Zucco

Directed by Roy Surette
Set and costumes designed by Anne-Séguin Poirier
Lighting designed by Ana Cappelluto
Stage managed by Luciana Burcheri
Stage manager assisted by Sarah-Marie Langlois
Director assisted by Mitchell Cohen

The St. Leonard Chronicles premiered in French at Théâtre Jean Duceppe de la Place des Arts in Montreal on December 18, 2014, and ran until February 7, 2015, then toured the province of Quebec from February 27 to May 9, 2015, with the following cast and crew:

TERRY	Émilie Bibeau
ROBERT	Pierre-François Legendre
CARMINE	Harry Standjofski
GINA	Sylvie Potvin
ELISA	Pauline Martin
DANTE	Claude Prégent
DORA	Béatrice Picard

Directed by Monique Duceppe
Set designed by Normand Blais
Costumes designed by François Barbeau
Lighting designed by Luc Prairie
Sound designed by Christian Thomas
Stage managed by Carol Gagné

CHARACTERS

TERRY PLESCIA, late twenties
ROBERT PLESCIA, her husband, late twenties
CARMINE (CARM) PATONE, Terry's father
GINA PATONE, Terry's mother
ELISA PLESCIA, Robert's mother
DANTE (DANNY) PLESCIA, Robert's father
DORA FANTINI, Elisa's mother

The parents are in their fifties or early sixties. Elisa's mom is in her early eighties.

SETTING

We are in St. Leonard, Montreal, Quebec. The time is NOW.

The set consists of a dining room, decorated in the latest style, with a touch – just a touch – of Italian St. Leonard kitsch (a chandelier, perhaps). Directly opposite we see a state-of-the-art kitchen, with stainless-steel appliances, the latest espresso maker, and modern cabinets.

We are in the home of Terry and Robert Plescia.

Note to Director: Dora dozes on and off throughout the play. A few indications have been made, but more can be added.

Note to Actors and Director: Dora, being the only one who came from Italy, can have a slight Italian accent. The rest were born in Canada so, while they may have an Italian "intonation," they do not speak with an accent.

Fade in on the dining room, where we find TERRY and ROBERT sitting around the table with Terry's parents, CARMINE and GINA Patone, and Robert's parents, ELISA and DANTE Plescia, along with Elisa's mother, DORA Fantini. They are finishing their antipasto (Prosciutto e Melone).

DORA

(*to the family*) April 1955. That's when we arrived here. It was full of snow and ice. As far as the eye could see: snow and ice. When we left the village in Italy, you could walk around in short sleeves, and here?

EVERYBODY

Snow and ice!

DORA

And not nice snow. Brown snow. So I thought to myself, if this is Montreal, me, I wanna go back home! But I knew we couldn't. When we finally get to my cousin's apartment – my cousin who I had never seen before in my life, that's where me and my husband were gonna live – when we finally get to the place, after what seemed like months at sea, there's these outdoor stairs to go up to the second floor where she lived. Narrow, made outta wood, and all curves. And I think to myself, this is Montreal? Who builds stairs outside, made out of wood, in a place that's still filled with snow and ice in April? Me, I wanted to go back home, but I knew we couldn't. So we get out of the car, get the trunk that carried all our belongings down from the top of the car, I take the baby – (*to ELISA*) your sister Anna – (*to the family*) in one arm, the front of the trunk with the other, my husband takes the back of the trunk, and we start climbing those *disgraziate* stairs. But me, I wasn't wearing winter boots. I didn't even know what winter boots looked like. So I'm slipping and sliding, and about midway up, I fall and I let go of the trunk. And the trunk hits my husband, and he lets go, and he slides all the way down along with the trunk, and he falls on his face on the ice. The neighbours were all looking, but do you think one of them moved their ass to come help us? No! Then I hear one of them say, "Stupid wops!" And another one, "*Maudits Italiens!*" I didn't know what it meant back then, but I knew by his tone it wasn't good. The first thing I heard when I got here. "Stupid wops." "*Maudits Italiens!*" Welcome to Montreal.

During Dora's speech, TERRY and ROBERT clear everybody's plates.

DANTE

And now they think we're all in the Mafia.

CARMINE

I wish! Me, I'd be rich if I were in the Mafia.

GINA

And you'd be dead.

DORA dozes off.

ELISA

Ma? (*to GINA*) I don't understand why she's falling asleep all the time.

DANTE

She's eighty-two.

ELISA

That's no reason.

GINA

Terry, you need any help?

TERRY

No, Ma, we got it.

GINA gets up and follows TERRY and ROBERT to the kitchen. ELISA does the same.

Cross-fade to the kitchen, where a pot filled with water and ravioli is boiling on the stove.

TERRY takes a raviolo from the pot and tastes it.

ELISA
I don't know what's wrong with my mother today.

GINA
She looks better than she did the last time I saw her.

TERRY
It's overcooked!

ROBERT
(*tastes it also*) Way overcooked.

GINA tastes it.

GINA
No, they're okay.

ELISA
Overcooked or not, so long as we eat.

TERRY pours the ravioli into a colander.

ROBERT
I hate mushy pasta.

TERRY drains the pasta.

GINA
They're not mushy, they're just soft.

TERRY takes the drained pasta and throws it in the garbage.

TERRY
We'll make another batch.

GINA
Why did you throw them out?

ELISA
Do you know how much they cost?

ROBERT
Yeah, Ma, we know, we paid for them. (*kissing his mom*) Go back to the dining room, we'll take care of it.

Cross-fade to the dining room. DORA is still snoozing. DANTE and CARMINE are in mid-conversation.

DANTE

. . . and then I hear "bam." "Bam, bam, bam." And the guy's dead.

ELISA and GINA return to their places at the table.

ELISA

Again with this Mafia?

CARMINE

In the restaurant you were eating at?

DANTE

No, in the *dépanneur* next door. I'm telling you, there's gonna be a Mafia war in Montreal like you never saw one before.

GINA

Mah, stop it. There's not gonna be a war.

CARMINE

What happened to the ravioli?

ELISA

It's gonna take a while longer.

CARMINE

But I'm hungry.

GINA

Eat your hand.

TERRY enters with a tray of champagne glasses and a bottle of champagne, followed by ROBERT with a birthday cake. DORA wakes up. TERRY and ROBERT break into a rendition of "Happy Birthday."

GINA

What's this now?

They stop singing.

TERRY

While we're waiting for the ravioli, we'll eat the cake.

ELISA

That's crazy, we can't have cake before ravioli.

DANTE

Come on, Elisa, let the kids have fun.

DANTE starts up "Happy Birthday" again. Everyone joins in. ROBERT puts the cake on the table. It is both Gina's and Dante's birthday.

Once GINA and DANTE have blown out all the candles, everyone (except DORA) applauds. During the next scene, TERRY cuts the cake, serves pieces to everyone, and they all eat.

GINA

Sixty! *Madonna,* I can't believe I'm sixty years old!

ELISA

(*to her husband*) Dante, I can't believe you're sixty either.

DANTE

You don't look it, Gina.

CARMINE

(*joking*) Yes, she does.

Everyone laughs, as ROBERT and TERRY serve some champagne.

ROBERT

Champagne?

GINA

Not too much for me. It gives me palpitations.

DORA

Gimme her portion, I can use some palpitations.

ELISA

Robert, not too much for Nonna.

ROBERT

(*serving his grandmother*) Come on, Ma, it's a party.

GINA
I can't believe I'm sixty.

CARMINE
You said that already.

DORA
You got more years behind you than you got in front of you!

TERRY
Ma, sixty is the new forty.

DORA
Sixty is sixty and seventy is seventy, and it's gonna go on like that until you die. (*to GINA*) Did you start farting yet?

TERRY and ROBERT are amused. The others are not.

GINA
Farting?

ELISA
(*trying to reassure everyone*) She'll fall back asleep soon.

DORA
I never used to fart, but when I hit sixty it's like my ass turned into a machine gun. I started farting at the hairdresser, at the grocery store, in church, in the bus. You name it, I farted in it. Fart, fart, fart, fart, fart, fart, fart.

ELISA
(*ignoring her mother*) What are the chances of you two being born on the same day in the same year?

DORA
I even farted in confession once.

TERRY
I propose a toast.

DORA
Stank up the booth so bad not even a bucket of Febreze could get rid of the stink. Fart, fart, fart, fart, fart!

CARMINE drinks his champagne.

GINA

Carm, why did you drink before she proposed a toast?

CARMINE

I was thirsty.

GINA

That's bad manners, you're not supposed to drink before the toast is proposed.

CARMINE

The toast was going to be for you and for Dante for being born on the same day in the same year. Right?

GINA

Right.

CARMINE

So, *salute!*

EVERYBODY

Salute!

They all drink, except CARMINE. We hear Nirvana's "Smells Like Teen Spirit" coming from the apartment upstairs. Everyone stares at the ceiling.

Beat.

ROBERT

Ricardo must be suicidal again, he's playing Kurt Cobain.

TERRY

He's always suicidal but he never actually shoots himself in the face. His music drives me crazy.

CARMINE

Is he ever late with his rent?

TERRY

No.

GINA

Then he's allowed to play his music all he wants.

ELISA

He's a nice guy. He took care of his mother and father until they died in the apartment.

GINA

How old is he?

TERRY

Late forties, I think.

ELISA

Too bad he never got married.

DORA

Gay!

ELISA

Again with this "gay." Just because a guy hasn't found the right girl doesn't mean he's gay. Your brother Tony never got married. He died at eighty-two, still single, and he wasn't gay.

DORA

Says you.

ELISA

He had a bunch of girlfriends.

DORA

And Tom Cruise had a bunch of wives, big deal.

CARMINE

Ricardo never got married because his mother was a miserable bitch who hated any girl he brought home.

GINA

Yeah, always blame the woman, even you. His father was no saint, you know.

TERRY

He's single now. He can bring home all the girls he wants, and he doesn't.

DANTE
Does he bring any guys in?

ROBERT
No.

DORA
Ten to one his mother had him fixed!

The music stops. No one reacts. The conversation does not skip a beat.

CARMINE
Hey, Danny, you watch the game last night?

DANTE
Why would I wanna watch the game? I know the Canadiens are gonna lose.

CARMINE
Bunch of idiots.

GINA
Can we please not talk about hockey on my birthday?

DANTE
Carm's right, they're a bunch of idiots. They lose early so they can go play golf. Back in the day, the players got paid nothing and they won, night after night after night.

DORA
Why is my glass empty?

TERRY fills Dora's glass.

CARMINE
Beliveau, Richard, Cournoyer – all French Canadians,
all excellent!

DANTE
Now we have all these other races playing hockey.

ELISA
Dante, since when are you so racist, even you?

DANTE

Who's racist? I'm stating a fact. When you want *pavé-uni* in your driveway, who do you call: a French Canadian or an Italian?

ELISA

An Italian.

DANTE

And when you want someone to win the Stanley Cup, who do you call, an Italian or a French Canadian?

ELISA

A French Canadian.

DANTE

(*having made his point*) *Ebbè?*

ELISA

Mah, shuddup.

DANTE

Vaffanculo.

DORA

After your father died my first lover was a French Canadian. His name was Fernand.

ELISA

Ma, you did not have any lovers after Pa died.

DORA

How would you know?

ELISA

You were living with me. I think I would've known if there was a "Fernand" sleeping in your bed.

DORA

What bed? We did it in the bathroom at *L'age d'or*.

TERRY

(*changing the subject*) I think it's time for the gift.

GINA
What gift? The cake is the gift.

CARMINE
Please, Gina, don't pretend like you don't want a gift.

GINA
No, Carm, I don't want a gift.

CARMINE
Then she'll get home and she'll say, "They didn't even get me a gift."

ROBERT
We got you both a gift.

TERRY
Actually, it's for all of you, even Nonna.

ROBERT
To show our appreciation for how much you help out around here.

TERRY gives an envelope to GINA and CARMINE while ROBERT gives an envelope to ELISA and DANTE.

GINA
(*opening her envelope*) Tickets to Miami Beach?

TERRY
Happy birthday, Ma.

DANTE
What's the Loews Hotel?

ROBERT
Where you'll be staying. It's right on the beach. Happy birthday, Pa.

ELISA
How much did this cost you?

ROBERT
It's a gift, Ma, you're not supposed to know how much it costs.

GINA

(*to ELISA*) I'll go on the Internet tonight and find out.

DANTE

No, no, no. This is too expensive.

CARMINE

You gotta be careful with your money.

GINA

You just got your new doors. You can't afford this.

TERRY

I think we're old enough to know what we can and cannot afford.

ELISA

Just because you have money now, doesn't mean you'll have money later. You spend, you spend, you spend, and next thing you know, you're poor.

ROBERT

(*losing it*) Jesus freaking Christ! Can't you just accept a freaking gift without making a freaking federal case out of it?

The parents are taken aback. ROBERT leaves for the kitchen. TERRY follows him.

Cross-fade to the kitchen, where the pot is starting to boil.

TERRY

Are you crazy, screaming like that, even you?

ROBERT pours himself a glass of wine from a bottle on the counter. TERRY puts the ravioli in the pot of boiling water.

TERRY

That's right, drink. That's gonna solve all the problems.

ROBERT

I should have emptied this bottle before they got here.

TERRY

I told you the Miami thing was stupid.

ROBERT
Don't pin this on me. You're the one who wanted to get them something different.

TERRY opens the fridge, sees something, screams, and shuts the fridge door.

ROBERT
What?

TERRY
Second shelf to the left.

ROBERT opens the fridge.

ROBERT
(*looking in the fridge*) What?

TERRY
Turnips!

ROBERT
You make me have a heart attack over turnips?

TERRY
Did we buy turnips?

ROBERT
We don't like turnip.

TERRY
Your mother bought the turnips, and *she* put them in there.

ROBERT
How do you know it was my mother and not your mother?

TERRY
Because your mother buys the turnip and my mother buys the fennel.

TERRY takes a turnip out of the refrigerator.

ROBERT
What are you doing?

TERRY

I'm gonna go shove this turnip down your mother's throat.

ROBERT

(*taking a fennel bulb from the fridge*) You do that, and this fennel goes up your mother's nose.

TERRY

That's fine with me.

ROBERT

Perfect!

The two head for the dining room. They stop abruptly. TERRY goes to the refrigerator and opens the door. ROBERT tosses the fennel in as if it were a baseball. TERRY does the same with the turnip and slams the door shut.

ROBERT grabs TERRY and the two kiss passionately.

ROBERT

I am so gonna screw the Italian out of you tonight!

Cross-fade to the dining room. The tickets are on the table. Everyone is silent until TERRY and ROBERT walk in.

TERRY

It shouldn't be too long now.

GINA

We were thinking about Wildwood.

TERRY

What about Wildwood?

CARMINE

I'll call my sister Rosa, she'll get you a full refund for the Miami tickets. She works at Sears Travel.

ROBERT

We didn't get the tickets at Sears Travel.

TERRY

Who gets tickets at a travel agency anymore?

CARMINE

Trust me, she can get a refund for anything, she's head manager there.

DORA

I hate Wildwood. All you do is walk up and down that stupid boardwalk and look at fat Americans eating fake Italian food.

GINA

(*to TERRY and ROBERT*) And you two can come too.

CARMINE

It'll be a nice family vacation.

TERRY

How is that a gift?

GINA

The cake is the gift.

ROBERT

Can't you let us do something nice for you?

DANTE

Tickets to Miami? That's your idea of nice?

CARMINE

What do we need to go to Miami for? Soon it's gonna be summer here too.

ROBERT

It's for the winter.

DORA dozes off.

DANTE

Winter? No, no, no – I'm not leaving Montreal in the winter. Who's gonna shovel the snow in front of our house?

GINA

No one's gonna go shovel the snow in front of the house, the thieves are gonna know we're not home, they're gonna break in, and they're gonna take off with everything, and we're gonna be left with nothing. It's like that, no?

ROBERT

You have a tempo. Why do you need to make mountains of snow if your car is in the tempo?

ELISA

He shovels the front yard. I feel like I'm in a cave when the front yard is full of snow.

DANTE

She feels like she's in a cave, and I'm the one who busts my back shovelling the snow.

ELISA

Mah, shuddup.

DANTE

Vaffanculo.

ROBERT

You won't see the snow, you'll be in the sun.

TERRY

We are *not* going to Wildwood.

GINA

Why not? It's nice.

ROBERT

Wildwood is an armpit.

DORA wakes up.

DANTE

You didn't think it was an armpit when we used to take you there every summer.

ROBERT

I was a kid!

DORA

When I was a kid the only place my parents took me was to pick the pockets of dead soldiers after there was an attack.

CARMINE

These two know nothing. They didn't live through the war.

TERRY

Neither did you.

ELISA

Our parents did, and trust me, it's the same thing.

DANTE

Not one supper went by without a death-by-death account of what they went through.

CARMINE

It was like reliving it every night.

GINA

It gave me a nervous condition.

ELISA

Maybe we can go to Old Orchard.

DANTE

The water's too cold in Old Orchard.

GINA

But the kids don't wanna go to Wildwood.

ROBERT

In Miami the water is like a Jacuzzi.

ELISA

That's too hot.

GINA

Me, I don't like it when the water's too hot in the ocean.

TERRY

You don't even swim in the ocean.

CARMINE

That's right. So why do you want us to go to Miami?

Stumped, TERRY leaves for the kitchen. ROBERT follows her.

Cross-fade to the kitchen. TERRY looks out the window, then at ROBERT.

TERRY

Seriously?!

ROBERT

What?

TERRY

(*pouring the ravioli into a colander*) What's today?

ROBERT

Sunday.

TERRY

And what happens tomorrow morning at six that you won't wake up for?

She tastes the ravioli. They're overcooked.

ROBERT

I didn't get to the recycling yet. What's the big deal? I'll do it later.

TERRY

Your only job around here is to do the garbage and the recycling, and guess who does it all the time? *Me!*

ROBERT

I said I would do it later!

TERRY takes the ravioli and throws them in the garbage.

Beat.

TERRY

Are we gonna end up like them?

ROBERT

Like who?

TERRY

Those four psychos out there.

ROBERT

No.

TERRY

We live in St. Leonard and we're arguing about recycling. We already *are* like them.

ROBERT

We're arguing *because* of them!

TERRY

(*shouting*) They're not the ones who didn't take out the recycling!

Beat.

I'm sorry.

Beat.

We're gonna get a divorce because of them!

ROBERT

You wanna divorce me?

TERRY

I never said that.

ROBERT

(*in a crescendo*) I'm not the one who brought up divorce.

TERRY

Stop putting words in my mouth. Jesus, you're just like your father!

ROBERT

And you're just like your mother!

TERRY

I am nothing like my mother!

ROBERT

And I am nothing like my father!

TERRY

The recycling will not take itself out!

After a beat, the two kiss passionately.

ROBERT

I am so screwing your mother out of you tonight! I'll go take out the recycling.

Cross-fade to the dining room. TERRY enters.

TERRY

Robert is taking out the recycling. It's gonna take a while longer. (*to DORA*) More wine?

DORA

You need to ask?

TERRY pours DORA a glass of wine.

ELISA

I like your wine this year, Danny. It tastes like vermouth.

DANTE

Your mother seems to like it a lot too.

ELISA

Mah, shuddup.

DANTE

Vaffanculo.

ROBERT enters.

CARMINE

You recycle?

ROBERT

Doesn't everyone?

GINA

Nah, it's too much trouble.

ELISA

What trouble? You separate the plastic and the paper from the rest of the garbage.

CARMINE

We don't have time for that.

DANTE

Because we do?

CARMINE

She just finished telling me you do it, so you do.

DANTE

We sometimes get up in the middle of the night to do the recycling because it's our civic duty!

CARMINE

I need my sleep. My job is very demanding.

ELISA

Because Danny's job isn't very demanding?

GINA

Elisa, please, you can't be comparing Danny's job with Carm's job now.

ELISA

Carm's a waiter.

CARMINE

(*defensively*) I happen to be partners with my brothers in a restaurant that was founded by my father.

DANTE

And what do you do most of the time?

CARMINE

I wait on tables.

DANTE

So what's the difference?

CARMINE
I *own* the tables.

ELISA
Danny is an accountant.

GINA
He works at Bonanza *supermarché*!

DANTE
I supervise the cash registers.

CARMINE
That doesn't make you an accountant.

ELISA
Do you know how many cashes there are at Bonanza?

DANTE
Fifteen.

CARMINE
It could be twenty, how does that make you an accountant?

ELISA
He counts the money when they're done. Isn't that what accountants do? They count money?

GINA
Yes.

ELISA
So he's an accountant.

GINA
Accountants don't count money from cash registers in grocery stores.

DANTE
You gonna tell an accountant what an accountant does?

CARMINE
(*to TERRY*) You and your stupid recycling, you see what you started?

TERRY

What's the big deal about separating your plastics and your paper from your garbage?

DORA

During the war in Italy we ate our garbage because there was nothing else to eat, and then whatever came out of us, we spread in our gardens to make our tomatoes grow faster so like that we wouldn't have to eat garbage again. Now *that's* recycling!

ELISA

She's got a touch of dementia.

CARMINE

How can anyone have a "touch" of dementia? You're either demented or you're not!

GINA

Me, I can't hear stories about the war anymore, I start to shake.

DORA

I lived through the war and *you* start to shake? Tell me how that works.

DANTE

We lived through our own wars when we were kids.

DORA

Did you ever have a gun pointed in your face?

DANTE

I was born in Little Italy and I was raised in Saint-Michel, what do you think?

ELISA

We all went to Catholic school with the nuns, that was war enough.

CARMINE

You were lucky to be with the nuns. Us, we were with the priests.

GINA

Because you think the nuns were nicer than the priests? You wish! Do you know what the nuns used to do to us? They used to put us in penance if we didn't go to church on Sunday mornings. They'd put rice on the floor and they would make us kneel on it for half an hour.

CARMINE

We got on our knees for the priests too.

DANTE

On our knees, heads on the floor, and they would whack us with belts, rulers, whatever they could find. I still have welts on my ass.

GINA

Do you know what it's like to kneel on rice for half an hour?

DANTE

Do you know what it's like not to be able to sit for two days? Father Di Salvio, that son of a bitch, if I had him in front of me now I'd punch him in the balls from here to Wildwood.

GINA

So when should we leave?

ROBERT

For where?

ELISA

Wildwood, where else?

ROBERT

(*exasperated*) You guys are . . . you . . . aaaaah!

ROBERT leaves for the kitchen. TERRY follows.

DORA

Do they have the runs?

Cross-fade to the kitchen. ROBERT and TERRY enter.

ROBERT

I'm not going to Wildwood. You can go if you want, but I'm not going!

TERRY tastes the ravioli.

TERRY

When are you gonna tell them?

ROBERT

That we're not going to Wildwood?

TERRY

No. What we were supposed to tell them tonight.

TERRY pours the ravioli into the colander.

ROBERT

Why me?

TERRY

You're the man of the house.

ROBERT decides to play a game of You're It to determine who will tell their parents the news. He points to himself, then TERRY, back and forth.

ROBERT

(*staccato*) "My-mother-and-your-mother-were-washing-the-clothes . . ."

TERRY

What are you doing?

ROBERT

Whoever is It tells them.

TERRY

That's ridiculous.

ROBERT

"My-mother-gave-your-mother-a-sock-in-the-nose. What-colour-was-the-blood?"

TERRY
This is dumb!

ROBERT
(*insisting*) "What-colour-was-the-blood?"

TERRY
Green.

ROBERT
That's a stupid colour, how can blood be green?

TERRY
I get to choose the colour I want, and I want *green*!

ROBERT
"G-R-E-E-N-and-you-are-It –

ROBERT continues, so that he is pointing at TERRY by the end.

– be-cause-I-said-so-and-the-king-and-queen-said-so-too." You're It!

TERRY
No, I'm not!

ROBERT
"The-king-and-queen-said-so-too." You're It.

TERRY
You're It. You're supposed to end with – (*pointing back and forth*) "and-the-king-and-queen-said-so."

This time it ends on ROBERT.

You don't add a "too."

ROBERT
You always add a "too."

TERRY
Maybe on your crappy street, but on mine, we never did.

ROBERT
You lived on the street next to mine!

TERRY
And that's not how we used to play it.

ROBERT
(*taking the ravioli and throwing it in the garbage*) It's the way everybody plays it all over the world! You're just chicken.

TERRY
Fine! I'll go tell them.

The two kiss passionately again.

ROBERT
I am so gonna screw the St. Leonard out of you tonight!

TERRY
That batch of ravioli was perfect, by the way.

Cross-fade to the dining room. ROBERT and TERRY enter.

TERRY
It's gonna be a while longer.

CARMINE
Are we ever gonna eat tonight?

GINA
Eat your cake.

CARMINE
I already had all kinds of cake already!

DORA
(*extending her glass*) My glass is empty.

TERRY pours DORA more wine.

GINA
Your wine came out real good this year. It tastes like vermouth.

DORA
She said that already – I thought I was the one who was supposed to be losing it.

ELISA

I'm the one who said that, Ma, not her.

DORA

Then you're the one who's losing it.

DANTE

The patience we need with this one.

ELISA

She has a touch of dementia.

CARMINE

Again with this "touch." She's either demented or she's not.

GINA

Carm, leave it alone.

CARMINE

How many people do you know who only have a "touch" of dementia?

ELISA

What do you have against me tonight? I repeat what the doctors told me, and they told me that she has a touch of dementia.

DANTE

If this is only a touch, what's she gonna be like when she's completely demented?

ELISA

Mah, shuddup.

DANTE

Vaffanculo.

DORA

This wine really does taste like vermouth.

GINA

Yeah, it's good. Me, I like vermouth.

DORA

My husband's used to taste like olive oil. That's what I like about Italian homemade wine: it always tastes like anything but wine, but it always gives me a good buzz. And so long as it gives me a buzz, it's good enough for me.

GINA

What do you need a buzz for, *signora* Dora?

DORA

Did you take a good look at my daughter? You think I could stare at that face all day long without a buzz?

ELISA

(*upset, speaking quickly, her tone crescendos the more upset she gets*) Yeah of course – I'm not Anna, the pretty daughter. But where's Anna now, ah? Is she taking care of you now, ah? No! Does she ever come to see you, ah? No! So that's your Anna. That's all she's good for, to be beautiful, and me to be ugly, but at least I'm here for you – and she's not!

Uncomfortable silence. A couple of beats.

GINA

(*all smiles*) How is Anna?

DANTE

Take a walk down to the corner of St. Lawrence and St. Catherine and you'll find out.

ELISA

That's not true!

DANTE

Everybody in this room knows about your sister.

ELISA

(*a little envious*) She lives in Laval. In one of those new developments where the streets are called like wine . . . You should see the house, it's like a mansion!

DANTE
With all the alimony she's collecting from the ex-husbands she screwed out of house and home, she should be living in a castle.

ELISA
Mah, shuddup.

DANTE
Vaffanculo!

DORA dozes off.

CARMINE
Is that near the new bridge?

ELISA
Yeah, not too far.

CARMINE
Don't talk to me about that bridge, it cost me a fortune.

DANTE
How come?

CARMINE
It's a toll bridge, but you don't put twenty-five cents in a basket like you used to – they take a picture of your car and you get a bill in the mail.

GINA
You're such an idiot.

DANTE
Those bastards at the City, they'll do anything to fill their corrupt pockets and keep our streets looking like Afghanistan.

CARMINE
(*to GINA*) Why am I the idiot?

GINA
(*to ELISA*) He took the bridge I don't know how many times, then he had a heart attack when he got the bill at home.

CARMINE
It's quicker to get to work, how was I supposed to know?

GINA

(*upset, speaking quickly, her voice crescendos too*) Because I told you, I read it in the paper. I know how to read, you know. But you, you never believe me, you never believed me, and you're never gonna believe me, and that's the story of our lives!

DORA

(*waking up*) *Minghia!* Give her some more vermouth, this party is finally coming alive!

ELISA

You know, if we wanna go to Wildwood we better book fast because everything goes quick.

TERRY

Oh my God! We're not going to Wildwood, you're going to Miami!

GINA

We're not going to Miami, you just got your bathroom done.

ROBERT

What does our bathroom have to do with Miami?

ELISA

You spent thirty thousand dollars on that bathroom. You can't afford Miami too.

TERRY

Again you're telling us what we can and can't afford?

DANTE

It would have been less expensive without the Jacuzzi.

CARMINE

And the fireplace. Who needs a fireplace in their bathroom?

DORA

In winter when it's cold and you're constipated a fireplace comes in very handy, thank you very much.

ROBERT

Are you gonna tell us how to redo our bathroom too?

DANTE

Did you ever pay a cent when you were living at home? Did we charge you rent or make you pay for the food you put in your mouth?

ROBERT

What does that have to do with anything?

DANTE

Before you got married all your paycheques went straight to your bank account, we never asked for a dime. And now what do you do? You spend all that money on a fireplace in your bathroom.

CARMINE

And a Jacuzzi!

TERRY

It's our money!

GINA

That you saved because we never made you pay a thing while you were living at home!

TERRY

So then that gives you the right to tell us what do in our home?

GINA

Pe' carità! Who tells you what to do?

TERRY

I never wanted a vegetable garden. I always hated vegetable gardens. I hate looking out my window and seeing all those goddamn wooden sticks that hold up the tomato plants.

GINA

So then why do you have one?

TERRY

Because you guys planted one!

CARMINE

But you like to eat the fresh tomatoes from the garden, ah?

ROBERT
If we want fresh tomatoes, we'll go to Jean Talon market and buy them.

DANTE
You think they're fresh?

ELISA
They're not, and they cost a fortune.

GINA
Here you get them for free. If you don't wanna pick them, we'll come pick them for you.

ELISA
Yeah, it doesn't take long.

TERRY
It's our backyard. You can't tell me what to do with my backyard!

CARMINE
But you can tell us where to go on our vacation?

TERRY looks like she's going to explode.

TERRY
You don't wanna go to Miami? (*taking the Miami tickets from the table, she starts ripping them to shreds*) Here! (*as she's tearing them up*) Don't go to friggin' Miami! Don't go! Don't go! Don't freaking go!

TERRY storms out, followed by ROBERT. There is dead silence.

Beat.

GINA
Me, I've never been to Florida.

ELISA
They say it's nice.

Cross-fade to the kitchen.

TERRY darts around the kitchen like a bat out of hell. ROBERT tries to calm her down.

TERRY

I need to break something, gimme something to break.

ROBERT

You tore the tickets up, isn't that enough?

TERRY

No. Gimme dishes, I need to break dishes.

ROBERT

Okay but you clean up the mess after you've broken them.

TERRY

You are *so* not supportive!

ROBERT

Can you calm down please?

TERRY

I can't calm down. My heart is racing, my blood is boiling, I'm having a heart attack, my blood pressure is exploding, and we're out of ravioli, so we're having spaghetti!

TERRY takes a package of spaghetti from the cupboard and dumps it in the pot.

ROBERT

That's nothing compared to how you'll feel after we tell them.

TERRY

We haven't told them yet?

ROBERT

No. We got sideswiped by the bridge, and my aunt Anna and I stopped paying attention at that point.

TERRY

So maybe I told them while you weren't paying attention?

ROBERT

No, but we have to tell them today. We put it off too long already.

TERRY
I am so exhausted! I don't have it in me anymore. I'm too old for this.

ROBERT
You're twenty-nine.

TERRY
I'm losing my will to live.

ROBERT
You're giving up? What kind of Italian are you?

TERRY
Aren't we supposed to be about *la dolce vita* and *dolce far niente*?

ROBERT
In Italy, they are. In St. Leonard, it's all about who has the nicest *pavé-uni* and stocking up on Javel when it's on special at the Pharmaprix. I'm going back in.

TERRY
I can't do it.

ROBERT
Together we can.

TERRY
I'm telling you I can't.

ROBERT extends his hand.

ROBERT
Come on, baby.

TERRY does not move.

ROBERT
Come on.

TERRY gives ROBERT her hand.

ROBERT
Take a deep breath.

TERRY takes a deep breath.

TERRY

Let's go.

Cross-fade to the dining room, where CARMINE and DANTE are Scotch-taping the tickets back together. DORA has dozed off.

GINA

We have a nice surprise for you.

ELISA

We put the tickets back together! Carmine hands Robert the tickets.

ROBERT

Why?

GINA

We felt bad.

TERRY

That's so sweet! So then, you're going?

CARMINE

No.

ROBERT

So why did you Scotch-tape the tickets back together?

DANTE

It was symbolic.

TERRY and ROBERT don't know what to say.

TERRY

(*calmly*) Thank you for your act of symbolism.

ROBERT

(*calmly*) It was very kind.

TERRY

Robert has something to tell you.

ROBERT

Yes, I do.

TERRY
We've been meaning to tell you for a while.

ROBERT
Yes, we have.

TERRY
And now is the perfect time.

ROBERT
Yes, it is.

GINA
You're pregnant!

TERRY
No, I'm not.

ELISA
You can't have children?

ROBERT
Of course we can.

CARMINE
Then why aren't you pregnant?

TERRY
Because I'm not.

DANTE
Why? Don't you wanna have kids?

ROBERT
We wanna have kids.

GINA
What are you waiting for then?

ELISA
Better to have your kids before thirty.

CARMINE
You don't wanna be old enough to be your kids' grandparents.

TERRY

I'm only twenty-nine!

DANTE

You're turning thirty next year, so you should get pregnant this year.

GINA

You'll like it. It's fun. I loved being pregnant. Didn't you like being pregnant, Elisa?

ELISA

It was the most beautiful time in my life, I felt so . . . (*at a loss for words*) full.

DORA

(*waking up*) I got pregnant on our wedding night. Your father threw me on the bed, threw himself on top of me, and *bing bang boom, bing bang boom, bing bang boom.* Done! It hurt like hell!

ELISA

Ma, please.

DORA

He didn't explain nothing to me. He just told me to lay there, and *bing bang boom, bing bang boom, bing bang boom* – I was pregnant. I didn't know nothing about being pregnant. I even asked my mother – I said, "Ma, how is thing gonna come outta me?" You know what she answered? "God will show you the way." But God showed me *'stu cazzo*. I thought the baby was gonna come out through my belly button. You can imagine my surprise when it didn't. Then, I'd barely stopped giving birth, and again, *bing bang boom, bing bang boom*. Every night. *Bing bang boom!*

ELISA

Ma, that's enough.

DORA

Even when I didn't want to. *Bing bang boom.*

ELISA

I said that was enough.

DORA
Barely finished doing the dishes – *bing bang boom.*

ELISA
I asked you to stop.

DORA
Barely finished breastfeeding the kids – *bing bang boom.*

ELISA
I swear to God, Ma.

DORA
Recovering from my operation – *bing bang boom!*

ELISA
(*losing it*) I can't *take* her anymore! She's gonna drive me *crazy*! She's already driven me crazy! Crazy crazy craaaazzzzzzzyyyyyyyyyyyy!

ROBERT
(*blurting out*) We're moving!

ELISA
What?

TERRY
That's our news. Tell them, Robert.

ROBERT
I already did.

ELISA
What do you mean, "moving"?

ROBERT
Moving.

DANTE
Moving?

TERRY
Moving as in leaving this house!

GINA
I don't understand.

ROBERT
We're selling the house and we're leaving.

ELISA
Did you get a new job and you have to move out of Montreal?

DANTE
Does it pay better?

CARMINE
You're going to Toronto?

GINA
Vancouver – I betcha they're going to Vancouver.

ELISA
Not Vancouver! That's a five-hour flight and I'm scared of airplanes!

ROBERT
We're moving to Beaconsfield.

A couple of beats, as everyone tries to take in the news.

DANTE
You got a better job in Beaconsfield?

TERRY
He didn't get a better job, he still has his stupid good-for-nothing lousy job. We're just moving out of St. Leonard!

GINA
Why?

ROBERT
Because we found a nicer house.

DANTE
How can you find a nicer house than this? This is a palace.

ROBERT
Palace? It's a duplex with a bachelor in the basement.

ELISA
Why would you wanna go to Beaconsfield? There's no Italians in Beaconsfield!

GINA
There's a couple of Italians in Beaconsfield.

ELISA
A couple but not a lot like in St. Leonard.

CARMINE
There's less and less Italians in St. Leonard.

DANTE
And more and more Arabs.

ELISA
I told you to stop being racist!

DANTE
(*making his point*) Were we all Italians when we bought our house in the seventies?

ELISA
Yes.

DANTE
Are we all Italians now?

ELISA
No.

DANTE
So stop calling me racist! I'm just stating facts.

GINA
It's still the best place to buy Italian food in Montreal.

DANTE
What are you gonna feed yourselves with in Beaconsfield?
Tim Hortons lasagna?

CARMINE
Are you running away from the Arabs?

TERRY
No-ah!

DANTE
That's why the Arabs are moving in, because the Italians are moving out.

ROBERT
There are Arabs in Beaconsfield!

CARMINE
Then why do you wanna go there for?

DANTE
You wanna live with Arabs, stay here.

TERRY
We are not racist.

GINA
Neither are *we*!

ELISA
You're the ones running away from the Arabs, not us.

TERRY
(*beginning to panic*) Oh my God, I can't breathe.

ROBERT
Stop being so melodramatic, even you.

TERRY
You see? That's why we wanna get out of St. Leonard. "Even you" has entered our vocabulary.

GINA
What's wrong with "even you"?

TERRY
We both have university degrees. I'm a notary, he's a financial adviser. We should not be using "even you" in a sentence.

ELISA

Why not?

ROBERT

Because it doesn't make sense. I don't even know what it means when I say it.

DANTE

Since when do you need to know what "even you" even means?

DORA

Ten to one, they'll run to the kitchen again.

TERRY

No! We're not running anywhere. We're tired of running – that's why we're moving. We found a nice detached two-storey cottage in Beaconsfield.

Everyone is shocked.

GINA

A cottage?

ELISA

You mean like a house?

CARMINE

What are you gonna rent in a cottage?

DANTE

Your bathroom?

ROBERT

That's the point! We won't have anybody living on top of us, and no one living under us.

DANTE

What's the point in having a house if you can't collect rent?

The song "Knockin' on Heaven's Door" can be heard coming from the upstairs apartment.

ROBERT

That's the point. (*to the ceiling*) I don't wanna hear music coming from upstairs anymore.

TERRY

We can even tell when he's getting a cold.

ROBERT

And I don't wanna know what he can hear us doing.

TERRY

Ewww-ah! I never even thought of that!

ELISA

So what do you want? Quiet?

ROBERT

Yes!

GINA

You wanna sit in your house and hear nothing?

ROBERT starts clearing the plates from the kitchen table.

TERRY

Isn't that what you're supposed to hear in your house? Nothing?

CARMINE

You're gonna go crazy hearing nothing all day long.

DANTE

You'll hear plenty of nothing when you'll be dead!

ROBERT

A house is supposed to be a sanctuary!

GINA

Me, I'd feel so lonely if I didn't hear Angelina Scarpaleggia walking in her high heels all day long.

CARMINE

I told her to wear slippers in the house, she's gonna ruin the ceramic.

GINA

I like hearing the high heels. It makes me feel like I have company at night.

TERRY

Why? Where's Pa at night?

GINA

At home, but he doesn't talk.

CARMINE

After thirty years of marriage, what's left to say?

ELISA

Nothing, unless you wanna argue.

DANTE

I'd rather hear my upstairs neighbour dancing around to Michael Jackson than listen to this one talk.

ELISA

Mah, shuddup.

DANTE

Vaffanculo.

ROBERT

You see? By not talking, that's what your marriage has come down to. You say "Mah, shuddup," he answers "*Vaffanculo.*" I've heard it all my life: "shuddup," "*Vaffanculo,*" "shuddup," "*Vaffanculo,*" "shuddup" –

DORA

(*waking up, raising her glass*) *Vaffanculo.*

ELISA

There's nothing wrong with our marriage.

ROBERT

I never said there was.

DANTE

Not in so many words.

TERRY

If you prefer listening to what your upstairs neighbour is doing, rather than talking to one another, I think there's something wrong.

CARMINE

I agree.

TERRY

(*to CARMINE*) I was talking about you!

GINA

There's nothing wrong with *our* marriage.

ELISA

What's that supposed to mean?

GINA

What's what supposed to mean?

ELISA

You emphasized "our" like there's nothing wrong with *your* marriage but there's something wrong with *ours*.

DANTE

There's nothing wrong with our marriage.

DORA

I knew a woman in Beaconsfield once.

ELISA

That was in Ville LaSalle, Ma.

DORA

It was Beaconsfield.

ELISA

(*exasperated, shouting*) It was Ville LaSalle, you never been to Beaconsfield.

DORA

(*shouting back*) I've been to Beaconsfield!

DANTE

(*yelling the loudest*) Name me one street in Beaconsfield, just one!

ELISA

Stop yelling at my mother!

DANTE

You people from Ville-Émard, you're all the same.

ELISE, DORA, and CARMINE are insulted.

ELISA

Here we go again.

DANTE

You say something, then, when you're asked to prove it, you can't.

DORA

I'm gonna smack him harder than the priest used to!

ELISA

Because you people from Little Italy, you're so much more intelligent.

DORA

Mixed marriages never work.

GINA

With all due respect, no one even knows you guys exist, okay?

CARMINE

We know we exist, that's what's important.

ELISA

The procession at St. John Bosco is twice as big as the one at la Difesa.

GINA

You don't know what you're saying.

CARMINE

It's a proven fact.

DORA

My friend Amalia married a guy from Montreal Nord. Hated each other's guts all forty-five years they were married.

TERRY

Forty-five years, that sounds like a successful marriage.

DORA

Back then nobody left nobody. You got married and that's it. (*clearly talking about herself*) You put up with your husband beating on you, cheating on you, getting drunk, throwing up in your face, and telling you he never loved you.

DANTE

Carmine, please, you can't compare what we have in Little Italy with what you have Ville-Émard.

CARMINE

Because we are the forgotten Italians!

GINA

Uffa! Again with that!

CARMINE

Our fathers worked in the gas factories and in all the other crap factories along the Lachine Canal, and there's not one sign in the old neighbourhood that even says, "This is where the Italian community was started in Montreal."

DANTE

Whoa! Whoa! Whoa! Where the Italian community was started? Little Italy is where the Italian community was started.

ELISA

We were here first.

DANTE

Maybe, but you didn't do anything of interest.

CARMINE

Because we didn't have Mafia money!

DANTE

(*insulted*) Repeat that because I don't think I heard right.

CARMINE
You heard right.

DANTE
I can't have heard right, because if I did, I'm gonna have to ask you to leave this house.

TERRY
This is my house, you can't ask anyone to leave.

DANTE
Your father just spit in my eye!

DORA
I wanted to leave my husband, but I was never allowed.

ELISA
Ma, please, you did not want to leave Pa.

DORA
I wanted to leave your father the day we got married.

DANTE
I'm still waiting for an apology.

CARMINE
You guys had *la Casa d'Italia,* you had Milano fruit store, you had Dante hardware store, and we had *'stu cazzo,* so I have nothing to apologize for!

ELISA
And now you show it off to all the tourists, like a three-ring circus. We don't show off in Ville-Émard.

GINA
What's there to show off, even you? Crack whores?

CARMINE
You take that back.

GINA
Who's talking to you?

CARMINE

All my life you made me feel inferior because I came from Ville-Émard and you were from Little Italy.

GINA

I didn't know you all your life!

ROBERT

What's the difference, you've all been living in St. Leonard forever!

ELISA

And now you wanna leave.

TERRY

You left *your* neighbourhoods.

CARMINE

That was different.

ROBERT

How?

DANTE

Our neighbourhoods were dumps.

ROBERT and TERRY are awestruck. Not knowing what to say, they take what's left of the cake from the table and leave for the kitchen.

DORA

Then I figured, how am I gonna get all my shit outta the house? And where am I gonna go? So I stayed with your father until he croaked one day while I was making lasagna. He just dropped dead in the kitchen. So I finished the lasagna, danced a little tarantella, and then I called 9-1-1, and that was the end of that.

DORA dozes off. The music stops.

Cross-fade to the kitchen. During this scene, TERRY empties the spaghetti into the colander, then dumps it in a bowl. She puts tomato sauce on the spaghetti while ROBERT gathers the plates and utensils.

TERRY

We're doing very well.

ROBERT

How are we doing well?

TERRY

We told them we were moving.

ROBERT

We should have run away in the middle of the night.

TERRY

We're not teenagers, Robert.

ROBERT

I'm telling you, Terry, we're gonna lose, and we're gonna stay in this wretched duplex until we die.

TERRY

How can we lose? They can't tie us to the house.

ROBERT

They'll find a way. They're in there right now, finding a way.

TERRY

Okay, then we trick them – we'll move while they're in Miami.

ROBERT

How is that different from running away?

TERRY

It's different because . . . (*she can't find the words*) It just is.

Cross-fade to the dining room. DORA has woken up. ROBERT and TERRY enter with the meal.

DANTE

Finally, food!

During this scene, ROBERT puts the plates and utensils on the table, and TERRY, the bowl of spaghetti. Everyone serves themselves, except for DORA, who is served by ELISA. They finally eat.

CARMINE

How did ravioli turn into spaghetti?

GINA

Always with the questions, you.

TERRY

We had a situation with the ravioli.

ROBERT

Next time we'll have ravioli.

DANTE

There's nothing like a good plate of spaghetti.

ELISA

I agree, who needs ravioli?

CARMINE

Not me.

The song "Parlami d'amore Mariù" ("Speak of Love to Me, Mariù") can be heard from the apartment above. DORA recognizes the song and starts singing along.

DORA

"Parlami d'amore Mariù, tutta la mia vita, sei tu!"

TERRY

You know this song, Nonna?

DORA

(*smiling from ear to ear*) He used to sing this to me all the time. "Speak of love to me, Mariù."

CARMINE

Your name is Dora.

GINA

Carm, shuddup.

DORA

(*singing*) *"Parlami d'amore Mariù . . ."*

CARMINE

I'm just saying, he shoulda been singing, "*Parlami d'amore,* Dora." No?

GINA

I said shuddup.

ROBERT

Nonno used to sing this to you?

DORA

Your nonno sang nothing to me. Osvaldo, he was the one who sang this.

ELISA

(*empathetic*) Ma, don't . . . please.

DORA

Osvaldo . . . I was fifteen years old, he was eighteen. We were so much in love. I'd sneak out of bed in the middle of the night to go meet him behind the church in the village. When my father caught us the first time he beat me so bad, but I didn't care. It was worth it because every smack in the face was a testament to my love for Osvaldo. Every time I snuck out, my father would catch me, and he'd beat me, and as he was beating me I'd say, "Hurry up and finish so I can go meet my Osvaldo."

ELISA

Ma, it's not good for you to talk about this.

DORA

(*upset*) What do you know what's good for me? I know what's good for me, and remembering the only man I ever loved in my life is good for me! (*nostalgic, melancholic*) The way he sang to me, the way he held me, the way he made love to me.

CARMINE

Minghia! At fifteen she was already making love, this one.

GINA

Shht!

DORA

He wanted to marry me. But my mother said he wasn't good enough because he was a *cafone* – a farmer – and our family ran the post office, so that made us superior to him.

Beat.

I would've been happy on a farm. I would've learned how to do everything there needed to be done. I could've had a happy life, if it wasn't for my mother!

ELISA

You had a happy life.

DORA

No! She killed my happiness. She had my brothers bring my Osvaldo to a field and they threatened to stab him in the eyes if he didn't stop seeing me. So I never saw my Osvaldo again! Never knew what happened to him. And then at sixteen years old my mother gave me to your father because he was coming to America and he was gonna be rich! Rich. Rich, don't make me laugh, rich! (*angry*) "Stupid wops!" "*Maudits Italiens!*"

Beat.

I still think of my Osvaldo every day of my life, and I will keep on thinking of my Osvaldo every day of my life until I die.

The music upstairs stops.

ELISA

You could've been just as miserable with Osvaldo!

DORA

So you're admitting I was miserable with your father?

ELISA

When were you miserable? He treated you like a queen!

DORA

If you think he treated me like a queen, you're the one with the touch of dementia, not me.

ELISA
I don't wanna talk about this anymore.

DORA
Poor Elisa – (*looking at DANTE*) always looking the other way. You never had the courage to face the truth.

DANTE
Why are you looking at me when you say that?

DORA
You know why.

ELISA
I said I didn't wanna talk about it!

DANTE
(*to DORA*) You never liked me.

DORA
Ever since I walked in on you and my daughter, no, I never liked you.

ELISA
Ma, please, not here.

GINA
(*laughing*) She walked in on you and Dante?

ELISA
She's got a touch of dementia.

CARMINE
And it worsened when she saw the two of you doing it.

ELISA
Let's change subjects, please.

DORA
(*staring at DANTE*) It was disgusting.

ELISA
(*shouting*) I said I wanted to change subjects. This is not something I want to talk about in front of my son!

CARMINE

What's the big deal? They're married. Terry, remember the time you walked in on me and your mother?

TERRY

I still have nightmares about it, thank you.

ROBERT

And I'll be having nightmares tonight, so if we can please . . .

DORA

(*blurting out*) I walked in on him and my Anna!

Everyone goes stone-cold quiet. DANTE gets up, shouting.

DANTE

I'm so fuckin' sick and tired of this shit!

ELISA

Calm down.

DANTE

She says anything that comes into her head, and I'm fuckin' fed up!

ELISA

That's because she's sick.

DANTE

She's not sick. She's a fuckin' drunk. When are you gonna admit that your mother is a fuckin' drunk! Even the doctor said it: there's no dementia! She's just a mean old lady with a drinking problem.

ELISA

(*dead serious*) She was perfectly sober when she walked in on you and my sister!

Everyone is shocked.

GINA

Oh my God, Elisa, is this true?

Beat.

ELISA

Why do you think we don't speak anymore? My sister is a slut. She's always been a slut, and men are weak. End of story.

DORA

If that's how you wanna look at it . . .

ELISA

I told you when it happened that's how I wanted to look at it. And I told you when it happened to keep it to ourselves. Why do you do this, Ma? Why do you always embarrass me in front of everyone?

DORA

Because I didn't raise you to be an idiot.

ROBERT

Nonna, please stop picking on Ma. She's been through enough with all the disgusting things Pa did to her.

DANTE

Nice thing for a son to say about his father.

ROBERT

Nice thing for a father to sleep with his sister-in-law.

DANTE

(*angry*) You know what? You wanna leave St. Leonard? Go! But you gimme my hundred thousand dollars back.

ROBERT

What do you mean?

DANTE

Our wedding gift to you was twenty-five percent of the cost of this house. You're selling the house, so I want my money back.

ROBERT

It was a gift, it didn't come with a return policy.

ELISA

Danny, please don't be ridiculous.

DANTE
I'm not being ridiculous.

GINA
That goes for us too. I want my twenty-five percent back too!

CARMINE
Gina, come on.

GINA
He has a point. You wanna go out on your own? Fine, go out and start from scratch. See how easy it's gonna be. Give us our one hundred thousand dollars back too!

TERRY
I don't believe this – you're punishing us for wanting to sell the house?

DANTE
"Punishing" is a strong word.

ROBERT
You want your money back? Fine. I'll make you a cheque, so like that you can go spend it on your whores.

ELISA
This is getting out of hand!

ROBERT
Oh come on, Ma, please. We all knew about him and *zia* Anna, and she wasn't the only one – he's been screwing around on you for as long as I can remember.

DANTE
What do you know about anything, you?

ROBERT
Don't even try to deny it. I'm the one who heard Ma crying in her bed when you got in at all hours of the night.

ELISA
He was working.

ROBERT

Why are you still defending him? Ma, please stand up for yourself.

DANTE

Yeah, Elisa, please stand up, tell everyone what an example of purity *you* are.

ELISA

(*uncomfortable*) We need to go home.

GINA

We're still eating.

ELISA

Ma's getting tired.

DORA

You go home, I'm having the time of my life.

ELISA

You keep on dozing off. You need your rest.

DORA

Now that we've established that I'm not demented and that I'm just a mean, rotten drunk, I don't need to go rest anymore. And why is my glass empty again?

TERRY gives her more wine.

ELISA

Okay, you guys don't wanna go home? Stay here – I'll walk.

GINA

We'll drive you.

CARMINE

We're not done eating yet.

GINA

The kids need to clean up. It's late and they go to work in the morning.

DANTE

Yeah that's right, go. Now that we're talking about Saint Elisa, everyone go home.

ELISA

(*to TERRY*) Leave the dishes, we'll come do them tomorrow.

TERRY

It's okay, we'll put them in the dishwasher.

GINA

They never come out good in the dishwasher, it's better to hand-wash. Come on, Carm.

Everyone gets up, except for DANTE and DORA, who has dozed off again.

DANTE

(*staring straight at his wife*) Giovanni Spadafora.

ELISA gets weak in the knees and sits down. GINA sits down too. CARMINE follows suit.

GINA

Are you okay?

ELISA doesn't answer.

ROBERT

(*worried*) Ma, you want some water?

ELISA remains quiet.

DANTE

Does that name ring a bell, Elisa?

ELISA

You promised on your mother's grave that you would never bring his name up ever again.

DANTE

I lied.

ROBERT
Who's Giovanni Spadafora?

ELISA
He's dead.

DANTE
But what was he when he was alive?

Dead silence in the room. A couple of beats.

ELISA
I'm not ashamed.

DANTE
Nice. You're not even ashamed.

ELISA
No! I'm not ashamed.

DANTE
You disgust me.

ROBERT
(*angry*) Don't talk to her like that!

ELISA
Don't raise your voice to your father.

ROBERT
He just said you disgust him.

ELISA
He's right to be disgusted.

DANTE
And she's not ashamed.

ELISA
No, I'm not ashamed.

DANTE
And you're not ashamed – because?

ELISA

(*looking DANTE straight in the eye, knowing that he knows*) Because I loved him.

DANTE

(*with a mixture of disgust and hurt feelings*) Nice.

Everyone takes in what just has been said.

Beat.

ROBERT

(*shocked*) Whoa. Whoa. Whoa. Whoa. Whoa!

Beat.

Whoa.

Beat.

Whoa! You loved who?!

ELISA

He was a butcher. You were too small to remember him.

CARMINE

Minghia!

GINA

Shht!

ELISA

It lasted a couple of years. We had made plans to run away together, but then one night he finished work and he went out through the back exit of the butcher shop, and he was run over and got crushed to death by a garbage truck in that filthy lane.

DANTE

A piece of garbage run over by a garbage truck. That's God's justice.

ELISA

(*this time she means it*) Shut up!

DANTE
(*he means it too*) *Vaffanculo!*

Beat.

GINA
You gotta be kidding me. Elisa, tell them it's a joke!

ELISA
I fell in love with another man, that's all. Dante found out, and he took revenge by sleeping with my sister and God knows who else. And he was right, because I hurt him. But I was in love.

ROBERT
And that's your excuse? You were in love. All these years you made me believe that Daddy was an animal, and it turns out that you were nothing but a –

DANTE
Don't say it, Robert. Please.

ELISA
A dirty slut. I heard it from your father enough times, and I can hear it from you too.

ROBERT
(*livid*) Where the fuck did I fit in this picture? Ah? Were you gonna leave me too?

ELISA
I don't know, Robert.

GINA
Oh *Madonna mia*!

ROBERT
You were gonna run away with your lover and leave me alone?

ELISA
I just finished telling you that I don't know.

ROBERT
I can't . . . I can't believe this.

TERRY
Babe, it's okay.

ROBERT
No, it's not.

ELISA
I don't expect you to understand.

ROBERT
What the fuck is wrong with you?

DANTE
Don't talk to your mother that way.

ROBERT
Is it because you were unhappy with Pa?

ELISA
No.

ROBERT
Then what was it? Were you going through a depression? Were you bored? Did you feel unfulfilled? Come on, Ma, I'm running out of reasons here!

ELISA
It just happened, Robert. I can't explain it. I don't even know myself. One minute he was serving me pork chops, and the next I was in bed with him. And then it just went on and on, until he died.

ROBERT
It just went on and on – that's your explanation?

ELISA
What do you want me to tell you? There is no explanation!

ROBERT
There's no explanation for fucking cancer, or fucking Alzheimer's, but you fucking a butcher while you were still my fucking mother – there has to be an explanation! (*after a beat, to DANTE*) And you? How come you're still with her after this?

DANTE

I forgave her.

ROBERT

By screwing around?

A shouting match ensues.

DANTE

It was the only way to deal with the pain. When I was screwing around, I forgot that my wife had fallen out of love with me and in love with the butcher!

ELISA

I never fell out of love with you!

DANTE

It's either-or, Elisa, you can't have it both ways.

Dead silence. DORA lets out a loud snore. Dead silence again.

GINA

(*completely out of sorts*) Has everybody gone nuts?! This is St. Leonard, for Christ's sake! We don't go around falling out of love with our husbands and having affairs!

GINA

We raise our kids, and we plant tomatoes, and we do the wash, and we hang our clothes outside even if we have dryers, especially the sheets because they smell better when they're hung outside, even if we know that we're next to Highway 40 and they're gonna be full of carbon monoxide, we still hang our clothes outside because that's who we are! And in the winter we put up our tempos, and in the summer we take them down. And we go to weddings, and we spend fortunes for our dresses and the gifts, and we gossip about the neighbours, and we bitch about our husbands – (*emphasizing*) but we do not have affairs!

TERRY

Ma, please calm down.

GINA

I will *not* calm down! There's a way of doing things here! It's what makes us different from the French and from the English and from the Portuguese and from everybody else. And she did not respect that way of doing things!

ELISA

You're angry because I did not respect some sort of imaginary St. Leonard protocol?

GINA

Yes! Yes, I'm angry. I never had an affair! I never even slept with anyone else except for this . . . (*referring to Carmine*) And now I find out that you were having an affair and your mother was being boffed when she was fifteen years old by some hunky farmer! And me? I don't know what it's like to have another man hold me. Make love to me. Make me feel special. This is St. Leonard! No one here is supposed to know what that's like!

CARMINE

What are you, jealous that she had an affair, even you?

GINA

Damn right I'm jealous! I'm sixty years old today! I been married for thirty-four years. Am I the only one who's been following the rules? How many other women in St. Leonard have been having affairs?

ELISA

How should I know? You think there's a club we all belong to?

GINA gets up.

GINA

I'm going home. Carm, let's go.

CARMINE

I can't believe you been thinking of having an affair all these years!

GINA

Because you never thought of sleeping with anyone else?

CARMINE

Never!

GINA

Not even you when you make love to me? You don't close your eyes and fantasize you're making love to someone else?

CARMINE

No!

DANTE

Then you're not normal.

CARMINE

You care to repeat that?

DANTE

We all think about sleeping with someone else at some point in our marriage. And we all think about someone else when we're nailing our wives.

CARMINE

(*to TERRY and ROBERT*) Have you kids ever thought about someone else when you're making love?

TERRY

I *so* don't wanna have this conversation with you.

CARMINE

Answer the question!

TERRY

Of course we do.

ROBERT

(*surprised*) Excuse me? Are you telling me that while I'm making love to you, you're thinking of someone else?

TERRY

What's thc big deal?

ROBERT

That's like cheating.

TERRY
No, it's not!

ROBERT
I am *never* making love to you again!

TERRY
You are such a child!

ROBERT
And you are such a skank!

Shocked, not knowing how to answer, TERRY leaves.

ELISA
Robert, go after her.

ROBERT
You never talk to me again!

GINA
Carm, we're going home.

CARMINE
Me, I'm staying here.

DANTE
Then we're going. Elisa, let's go.

ELISA
This is all my fault.

DANTE
Yeah I know, now let's go.

ELISA
(*to DORA, who is sound asleep*) Ma, come on, we're going.

DORA is still sound asleep. TERRY enters with a laptop.

ROBERT
What are you doing with my computer?

TERRY
I'm the skank? We'll see who's the skank in this marriage!

TERRY puts the computer on the table and opens it.

ROBERT

Don't fuck around, all my work is in there.

TERRY

All your work, yeah. Let's take a look at your "work." (*hands on the keyboard*) Let's see – Robert's folder. Open. Rescued Items from Macintosh Hard Drive. Open. And – play!

TERRY has opened a porn movie on Robert's hard drive. Sexual moans are heard. Everyone is shocked. The moans wake up DORA.

ROBERT closes the computer. TERRY re-opens the computer, and moans are heard again. ROBERT closes it. TERRY reopens it, moans are heard. ROBERT closes it again. After a beat, DORA opens the computer. ELISA shuts it.

DORA falls asleep again.

TERRY

You have over one hundred porn movies on your hard drive! Man on woman, woman on woman, three-way, four-way, any-way – you name it, it's there!

ROBERT

Jesus Christ, you even counted? It's no big deal, it's just porn! Everybody watches porn! It's a proven fact! Plus I need some stimulation, I'm the one who does all the work while you just lay there!

TERRY

(*beyond insulted*) Lay there? Lay there? I do *anything* but just lay there.

ROBERT

You just lay there while you're thinking of someone else. Who the fuck are you thinking about anyway?

GINA

(*shouting*) How did my birthday turn into a scene out of Sodom and Gomorrah, that's what I wanna know!

CARMINE
Who the hell did you wanna have an affair with anyway?

ELISA
(*to DANTE*) You see what you started?

DANTE
Before you said it was you, now it's me? I'm not the one who slept with the butcher.

ELISA
No, even better, you slept with my sister.

ROBERT
Who was this butcher anyway? I don't even remember a butcher shop in our neighbourhood.

DANTE
It was some butcher in *Ville à Marde.*

CARMINE and ELISA gasp.

CARMINE
(*incensed*) Would you care to repeat that?

DANTE
Ville à Marde! Città di merda! City of shit!

Livid, CARMINE gets up and leaves.

GINA
Where's he going, that one now?

ELISA
(*to DORA, who is still sleeping*) Again she fell asleep. What's wrong with her tonight? Ma, for the last time, wake up, we're going home!

CARMINE re-enters carrying a cardboard box filled with bottles of wine.

CARMINE
Ville à Marde, ah? *Città di merda,* ah? You wanna see what real shit looks like, ah?

CARMINE puts the box on the floor.

DANTE

That's my wine!

CARMINE clears the table with his arm with one fell swoop. Glasses, dishes, spaghetti, and laptop go flying and land all over the dining room.

CARMINE then picks up the box and plunks it down on the table. He takes out two jugs of homemade wine.

CARMINE

This isn't wine! This is liquid shit! And there's a million boxes of this liquid shit down in the canteen.

DANTE

(*to ROBERT and TERRY*) You haven't been drinking my wine?

CARMINE

No, they haven't been drinking your wine.

DANTE

Then why do you keep it?

ROBERT

We didn't wanna insult you.

DANTE

By hiding the bottles in the canteen you're not insulting me?

CARMINE

You're insulting them, because your wine doesn't taste like vermouth – it tastes like shit!

CARMINE opens a bottle, drinks straight from it, and spits the mouthful out. Everyone takes cover as best they can as it splatters all over the place.

CARMINE

(*shouting*) Shit!

CARMINE takes another gulp – and then spits it out.

CARMINE

(*shouting louder*) Shit!

CARMINE takes another gulp and spits it out.

CARMINE

(*shouting*) Shit!

Once more, with more oomph, more wine, and a spectacular evacuation.

CARMINE

(*shouting loudest*) Shit! Shit! Shit! Shit! Shit! Shit!

GINA grabs the bottle from Carmine.

GINA

Basta!

CARMINE is out of breath. GINA gently calms him down. The rest are looking around the room, which looks like a tornado has hit it: broken dishes, broken glass, spaghetti, and expelled wine all over the place.

DORA has slept through the whole thing.

After having calmed him down, GINA takes her husband by the hand.

GINA

(*smiling*) It was a lovely evening. Thank you for the cake.

CARMINE

And the tickets to Las Vegas.

TERRY

Miami.

DANTE

I think it's time to go now.

ROBERT

I think that's a good idea.

ELISA
Ma, wake up, we're going home.

GINA
How could your mother sleep through all this?

ELISA
She's a little deaf. (*loudly*) Ma, I said wake up, we're going home!

CARMINE
Me, I never been to Las Vegas.

DANTE
(*loudly*) Old lady! Wake up or else you're gonna stay in that chair until the rest of your days!

GINA
How come she's not waking up?

ELISA
(*a little panicked*) Ma?

ROBERT
Nonna?

TERRY
Nonna!

GINA
Signora Dora?

CARMINE
Wake up!

DANTE
Old lady!!

ELISA
(*shouting*) Ma! (*shouting louder*) Ma! (*loudest, realizing DORA is dead*) Maaaaa!!

Blackout.

This transition should be made as quickly as possible. Music plays during the little "break."

Fade in on the kitchen as ELISA, DANTE, CARMINE, GINA, ROBERT, and TERRY enter the room. They are all dressed in black, having just returned from Dora's funeral.

TERRY
Does anyone want coffee?

GINA
Are you having any?

TERRY
No, but I can make some.

ELISA
No, we don't want any.

TERRY
Still I can make some.

ROBERT
Nobody wants coffee.

TERRY
I want some.

DANTE
If you're making some . . .

GINA
Not too strong, we're all agitated.

TERRY starts making regular drip coffee.

CARMINE
You're making regular coffee?

ROBERT
We're out of espresso.

DANTE
What Italian is ever out of espresso?

ROBERT
We haven't had time to do the groceries.

GINA
I don't know why deaths have to be a three-day affair. When I go, just bury me and that's it.

CARMINE
Where? In the tomato garden, even you? You don't want a funeral?

GINA
No. I hate funerals. They make me sad. Just bury me and that's it.

CARMINE
So what, they make you sad? You're not gonna be there.

GINA
I said just bury me, and that's it. Can't I even do what I want in my own funeral?

CARMINE
No!

TERRY takes an envelope out of a drawer.

TERRY
Nonna left us something.

GINA
What something?

ROBERT
When she turned eighty, she gave us this envelope to be opened on the day of her funeral.

ELISA
And you waited until now to open it?

ROBERT
(*snapping at her*) That was the point. And who said you could talk to me?

ELISA starts to cry. DANTE consoles her.

DANTE

Can't you have a little compassion for your mother on this day? Don't you see how short life is?

ROBERT

Nonna was eighty-two. It's not that short.

ROBERT opens the envelope. He takes out a piece of paper – a note from DORA – and a small digital voice recorder.

ROBERT

(*reading the note*) "Kids, Dora here. If this isn't the day of my funeral, I will put a curse on you from my grave and your lives will be so miserable you'll wish to God to be in my place if I'm really dead."

DANTE

(*to ELISA*) At least we know for sure your mother really wrote that.

ELISA smiles.

ROBERT

(*reading*) "Now you idiots shuddup and listen to what I recorded."

ROBERT turns on the digital recorder as a special goes up on DORA, who is sitting on a rocking La-Z-Boy chair that has been set up somewhere onstage where the mess made in the previous scene is not visible. An old-style record player sits next to the chair on a small table. DORA speaks the following lines from her chair. Although the family only hears her voice on the recorder, the audience can see her.

DORA plays around with the digital recorder and turns it on.

DORA

Testing, testing, one, two, three. This piece of crap better work because it cost me one hundred and fifty bucks. You see, Elisa? Your partially demented mother can get herself to Future Shop and buy herself a digital recorder. By the way, if you're still looking for the two hundred bucks missing from your purse, now you know where it went.

Everyone laughs.

DORA

So I'm dead. That's pretty much what I thought would happen. You're born, you live, you die, end of story. And now I will share all my wisdom, all my life lessons, and everything a dead person is supposed to know, to annoy the living. First off – (*can't think of anything*) what I'd like to say – (*looking for her words*) the most important thing in life is – (*still searching, then finally*) Dammit, I got nothing! Isn't that a kick in the balls? After eighty years you'd think I'd have something, but no, I got nothing. Well, I guess we'll leave it at that. Don't wanna waste anymore of your time. I got nothing. But wait, I must have something. The only thing I'm feeling right now is . . . The only thing I know right now is that . . . (*after a beat, changing from upbeat to melancholic*) The only thing I know is that . . . I'm very sad.

I'm eighty today and even if I die at a hundred, it doesn't change the fact that it's still very sad. I'm not ready to go. After you reach a certain age you'd think that one would be ready, but I'm not. Not now, not in twenty years, not ever. I mean, who knows what's on the other side? Who knows if there *is* another side? There's supposed to be a tunnel and then light, but I don't like tunnels. That's why I never took the metro. And I don't wanna go, I wanna stay with you because . . . (*after a beat, on the verge of tears*) I'll miss you guys. I'll miss telling you my stories that make everybody cringe, and I'll miss getting drunk on cheap wine, and I'll miss aggravating you, Elisa, and I'll miss you, Dante, even though you always got on my friggin' nerves, and my beautiful Robert, knowing that I'll never see you again, it kills me! Which is a good thing, I guess, because I'm dead. And Terry, sweet Terry, always so kind to me, always giving me more wine even when that idiot daughter of mine told you not to. I'll miss all of you so much! I'll miss our parties, and our Sunday dinners, and everything else that goes with being alive! Goddammit, I'll even miss farting!

Beat.

Dammit! This tape was supposed to be full of wisdom by a wise old lady, but I'm not wise, and I'm not old. My mother was old – even though in reality I am older than she was when she croaked – my mother was the old lady, not me. (*on the verge of tears*) And I'm so scared. So scared of where I'll be when you hear this. Chances are, I'll be nowhere. I'll be nothing. And you'll never see me again –

DANTE starts to cry like a baby, much to everyone's surprise. ELISA consoles him.

DORA

– and even worse, I'll never see you guys again! Never! Ever! Again! (*composing herself*) Unless there really is a heaven and a hell – then I'll drop by hell from time to time to come visit you guys.

Everyone snickers.

DORA

Elisa and Dante, I would like to thank you for not closing me up in a home those last couple of years, and for making me feel like I was part of the world, part of the living, part of your family.

ROBERT runs into his mother's arms.

DORA

(*becoming emotional again*) I would like to thank you for putting up with a partially demented old woman. Thank you . . . Thank you . . . Thank you . . . *Grazie!* (*regaining her composure*) So that's the end of that. I love you all. A lot. And now, it's time to call it a day. (*after a beat*) Actually . . . It's time to call it a life. (*after a beat, with tenderness*) Stupid wops. *Maudits Italiens.*

Blackout on DORA. The recording stops.

ELISA

Why did she have to wait until after she was dead to tell us she loved us?

CARMINE

She didn't mention us at all.

GINA
I love you, Carmine!

CARMINE
What's gotten into you?

GINA
I don't wanna wait until after I'm dead to tell you that I love you.

CARMINE
I love you too, Gina.

The two kiss tenderly.

Beat.

DANTE
And I love you, Elisa.

ELISA
And I love you, Dante.

ROBERT
And I love you, Pa.

Beat.

ROBERT
And I love you too, Ma.

ELISA
I love you, Robert.

GINA
Terry?

TERRY
I love you too, Robert.

GINA
I meant us.

TERRY
I love you too, Ma and Pa.

GINA

We love you too, Terry.

ELISA

Robert, you have to sell this house. Nonna died here, you can't live in the same house Nonna died in. You'll see her in that dining room, crouched over all the time.

ROBERT

(*emotional*) The last thing she saw was my porn.

DANTE

You have to sell.

ROBERT

We have to sell.

CARMINE

Don't hire a moving company.

DANTE

They'll rip you off.

TERRY

We won't hire a moving company.

CARMINE

We'll help you move.

GINA

Elisa and me, we'll do the boxes.

ROBERT

We don't have boxes.

ELISA

There's a place I know you can buy boxes for twenty-five cents each.

DANTE

And that thing I said about wanting the down payment back, forget it, I was just being an ass.

TERRY
You were just being an ass.

GINA
Me too. A big dumb ass.

ROBERT
A big dumb ass.

CARMINE
The biggest dumb ass.

GINA
They got the picture.

CARMINE
You can get a good price for this house.

ROBERT
A really good price.

GINA
My neighbour in the back? She sold her duplex, not even renovated, for five hundred and twenty-five thousand.

ROBERT
Five hundred and twenty-five thousand!

DANTE
My neighbour from across the street, he went to Miami one winter, and he never came back.

ELISA
I don't blame him. I wouldn't miss St. Leonard one bit.

GINA
Not one bit.

CARMINE
That settles it! We're *all* going to Miami.

Dead silence.

Beat.

ROBERT

(*blurting out*) I don't wanna sell the house!

TERRY

What?

ROBERT

I don't wanna leave St. Leonard.

TERRY

What is wrong with you?

ROBERT

I don't wanna leave St. Leonard, what can I tell you?

TERRY

What do you mean, you don't wanna leave St. Leonard?

ROBERT

It's like Nonna said on the tape, I don't wanna go somewhere where I'll be cut off from real life. So I wanna stay right here. I wanna see old men shovelling snow in the winter, from the first snowflake to the last, and I wanna see them watering the sidewalks in the summer even though they'll never get them clean. I wanna walk down the street on a Sunday and see little old ladies going to church. And come September, I wanna make tomato bottles. I like making tomato bottles. And they won't make us make tomato bottles in Beaconsfield. I think there's a city bylaw against it. So I don't wanna go die in Beaconsfield! I wanna live in St. Leonard!

TERRY is livid.

TERRY

Well fuck me!

ROBERT

I'm sorry, babe.

TERRY

Fuck! Fuck! Fuck! Fuck! Fuck! Fuck! Fuck! Fuck me!

ROBERT

I said I was sorry, babe.

TERRY

Fuck! Fuck! Fuck! Fuck! Fuck! Fuck! Fuck! Fuck me!

Beat.

Don't be sorry!

Beat.

I don't wanna leave St. Leonard either! Shit! What is it with this place? It's like once you move in here or once you're born here, you can't leave. It's almost like it's surrounded by a barbed-wire fence, and if you try to get out, you'll be shot by some old fascist left over from the war! And you know what's worse?

ROBERT

Nothing can be worse than not wanting to leave St. Leonard!

TERRY

I wanna go to Wildwood!

ROBERT

You too?

TERRY

Me too!

Beat.

DANTE

(*angry*) Oh! Mah, you're really busting our balls now you know that?

ELISA

(*also angry*) You move, you don't wanna move.

CARMINE

(*ditto*) You don't wanna go to Miami, you wanna go to Wildwood.

ROBERT

Going to Wildwood in the summer and living in St. Leonard the rest of the year is our heritage!

TERRY

(*to her parents*) Why do you wanna us to move away from our heritage?

CARMINE

We want you to move away? We're not the ones who found you the house in Beaconsfield!

GINA

You two have gone completely crazy!

ELISA

And you're driving us nuts too!

The lights go up on the La-Z-Boy chair where DORA was sitting, now empty. During the following exchange, DORA enters, with a vinyl forty-five in her hand.

ROBERT

Of course we're crazy! We're Italian! Everyone in this room is crazy!

ROBERT

And we need to stay in a place where everybody else is crazy too: St. Leonard! Because in St. Leonard we're considered sane even though we're crazy!

TERRY

But in Beaconsfield, we're crazy, period!

GINA, CARMINE, ELISA, and DANTE are at a complete loss for words. DORA puts the record on. "Parlami d'amore Mariù" starts to play. DORA sits and listens to the song.

DANTE

Uffa! Again, this one upstairs with his music! I thought you wanted to get away from this.

CARMINE

This guy has no respect! He knows we just came back from a funeral. He was even there!

GINA

(*realizing*) Isn't that the song?

Everyone goes quiet.

ELISA

"Parlami d'amore Mariù." The song Osvaldo used to sing to Mamma. Every afternoon at around three, she'd sneak into her room and put this record on, and lock the door. Every day, over and over, for about an hour.

Everyone gazes in Dora's direction (they don't actually see her). DORA is standing now. With her eyes closed, she is gently swaying to the song.

ELISA

What was going through her head, I don't know, and I never bothered to ask. (*after a beat, realizing*) What time is it now?

Blackout on ELISA, DANTE, CARMINE, GINA, TERRY, and ROBERT.

DORA sways softly to the music for a couple of beats. She then starts to cry as though she had just lost Osvaldo. Her sobs come from deep within her soul. The pain is still raw after all these years. She cries for what could have been and what should have been. She cries and cries and cries as the song fades out. She continues to cry for a couple of beats as the lights fade out.

Blackout.

THE END

PHOTO BY MATHIEU DUPUIS

ABOUT THE PLAYWRIGHT

Steve Galluccio began his career in the Montreal underground theatre scene in 1990. He burst into the mainstream with *Mambo Italiano,* one of the most successful plays in Canadian theatre history. The play was made into a feature film, which became an international hit, sold in more than fifty-three countries. Galluccio followed *Mambo Italiano* with the Gemini Award–winning TV series *Ciao Bella*. Filmed in both French and English, *Ciao Bella* played on CBC Television and on Radio-Canada and was broadcast in Europe and in the United States.

Galluccio's second feature film, *Surviving My Mother,* won the audience favourite award at the Montreal Film Festival and has featured in many prestigious film festivals the world over. Galluccio's third feature, the bilingual *Funkytown,* opened in January 2011 and grossed more than $1.5 million. *In Piazza San Domenico,* Galluccio's ninth play, was the number-one comedy in Montreal in the fall of 2009, selling out most of its extended run. The play was performed in Germany in 2011. In 2012, Galluccio released his first non-fiction book, *Montréal à la Galluccio,* a whimsical guide to his beloved hometown.